Adult Golf J

The Ultimate Collection of R~~ude ~~~ ~~~~

Published by Glowworm Press
7 Nuffield Way
Abingdon OX14 1RL
By Chester Croker

Adult Golfing Jokes

These rude jokes for golfers will make you laugh. Some of these adult golfing jokes are rude, some are risqué and some are racy, and they are not for the easily offended.

If you like dirty golf jokes, you are in for a treat, as these funny adult golfers jokes will soon have you in stitches.

These dirty golfing jokes are ideal to tell at society days, club matches, tours at home and abroad and so on, and you can easily change the names in the jokes to suit your own story telling purposes.

We hope you enjoy this collection of the very best adult golfing jokes and stories around.

DEDICATION

This book is dedicated to James Day, who has one of the funniest golf swings you are ever likely to see.

He is the man that once told me he takes 17 holes to get warmed up.

He is the man that once told me that one good shank deserves another.

He is the man that taught me that no matter how badly you are playing, it is always possible to play worse.

He is the man who, after he missed a short putt, told me it was because his ball was scared of the dark.

For Jim, one birdie is a hot streak.

Jim, you are the inspiration behind this book, and I salute you.

FOREWORD

When I was approached to write a foreword to this book I was very flattered.

That is until I was told that I was the last resort by the author, Chester Croker, and that everyone else he had asked had said they couldn't do it!

I have known Chester for a number of years and his ability to create funny jokes is absolutely incredible.

He is quick witted and an expert at crafting clever puns and amusing gags and I feel he is the ideal man to put together a rude golfing joke book. I do remember him once telling me that to see something really funny, I should just watch his short game.

He will be glad you have bought this book, as he has an expensive lifestyle to maintain.

Enjoy!

Major Mulligan

Table of Contents

Chapter 1: Rude Golfer Jokes

If you're looking for funny adult golfing jokes you've certainly come to the right place.

In this book you will find rude and risqué, dumb and dirty golfer jokes that will make you laugh out loud.

There are a few dirty one-liners to start with, some quick-fire question and answer themed gags, many story led jokes which are easy to remember for your own story telling purposes, plenty of rude golf gags and as a bonus some cheesy pick-up lines for golfers.

You can easily change the names in the jokes to suit your own story telling purposes.

These jokes are ideal to tell at golf meetings, society days, club matches, tours at home and abroad etc.

Chapter 2: One Liner Rude Golf Jokes

The other day I was playing golf and I hit two of my best balls. I stepped on a rake.

A wife walked into the bedroom and found her husband in bed with his golf clubs. Seeing the astonished look on her face, he calmly said, "Well, you said I had to choose."

Never forget, it's not the size of your club that counts, it's how many strokes you take.

I met an ambidextrous lady golfer yesterday. She swings both ways.

A male golfer is often a confused soul who talks about women when he's playing golf, and about golf when he's with a woman.

Golf is like life - you go for the green, but end up in a hole.

Chapter 3: Q&A Rude Golf Jokes

Q: What do golf and sex have in common?

A: *They're two things you can enjoy even if you're not very good at either of them.*

Q: Why is the game called "golf"?

A: *Because all the other four letter words were already taken.*

Q: What is the difference between a lost golf ball and the G-spot?

A: *A man will spend 3 minutes looking for a lost golf ball.*

Q: What do you call a dipsy blonde golfer with an IQ of 125?

A: *A foursome.*

Q: How can you tell which golfer is a womanizer?

A: *He's the one getting his balls cleaned.*

Q: What do you call a dumb blonde at a golf course?

A: *The 19th hole.*

Q: How do you know a golfer is cheating on his wife?

A: *He puts his driver in the wrong bag.*

Q: What do you do after a round on a hot sunny day?

A: *Wash your balls.*

Q: What did the golfer say after performing yoga?

A: *"Damn, my shaft is all bent."*

Q: What do four-putting and masturbation have in common?

A: *You're ashamed of what you have done but you know it will happen again.*

Q: Why did the blonde golf pro cheat on his wife?

A: *Because he thought he needed to play around every day.*

Q: What do you call Jessica Alba joining you and your buddies for a round of golf?

A: *A Fantastic Four-Some.*

Q: What did the Mormon say to his golfing buddies?

A: *"After 18 holes, I can barely walk."*

Chapter 4: Rude Caddie Jokes

A young caddie came running into the pro shop saying, "Mrs McDonald has been stung by a wasp."

The pro asked where and the caddie replied, "Between the first and second hole."

The pro coolly said, "Tell her that her stance is too wide."

A golfer has been slicing his drives on every hole.

He asks his caddie if he has noticed any obvious reason for his poor tee shots, to which the caddie replies, "Yes, there's a piece of sh*t on the end of your driver."

The golfer picks up his driver to clean the club face, at which point the caddie says, "No, the other end."

Shamus was a reasonable golfer but he had a justifiable reputation for being very poor with his bunker shots.

He has even told his golfing buddies that he has nightmares about sand.

One day, playing a well-known links course, he hired a caddie who became exasperated at Shamus's shameful efforts in various sand traps during the round.

On the eighteenth hole, Shamus played his ball into a deep fairway bunker and he asked his caddie what club he should use.

His frustrated caddie replied, "Never mind the f*cking club. Just take plenty of food and water."

Chapter 5: Short Rude Golfer Jokes

A guy stood over his tee shot for what seemed an eternity; looking up, looking down, measuring the distance, figuring the wind direction and speed.

Finally his exasperated partner says, "What's taking you so long?"

The guy answers, "My wife is up there watching me from the clubhouse. I want to make this a perfect shot."

His partner says, "Forget it, man. You don't stand a snowball's chance in hell of hitting her from here!"

Four golfers were introducing themselves to one another on the first tee.

One asked, "How do you feel about a lot of swearing and moaning?"

"It doesn't bother me at all," answered another.

"Good," replied the golfer who has asked the question, "In which case would you phone my bitch of a wife and tell her where I am."

Glynn and Joe emerged from the clubhouse to tee off at the first hole.

"Anything the matter, mate?" Joe asked his buddy.

"I can't stand the club pro," Glynn replied, "he's just been trying to correct my stance."

Joe soothed, "He's only trying to help your game."

Glynn replied, "Yeah, but I was using the urinal at the time."

An Irish golfer drove his ball into his German neighbor's garden. He went to ask for his ball back and the neighbor said, "Sorry, old German custom dictates that possession is nine tenths of the law."

The Irish guy replied, "Well mate, an old Irish custom is that we take it in turns to kick each other in the bollocks, me first, and the last man standing gets to keep the ball."

"OK" says the German.

The Irishman then kicks him in the balls as hard as he can and then says, "You can keep the ball, Fritz."

A blonde was receiving golf lessons, but she was not doing well and kept sending the balls wide into the trees.

The instructor said, "I think the problem is with your grip on the club, you should grab it more gently. Just imagine that the golf club is a man's cock."

The blonde thought about this for a moment, picked up the club and then hit the golf ball.

It flew beautifully straight and long.

The instructor was amazed and said, "What a great shot. Now, next time, try gripping the club with your hands and not with your mouth."

My buddy looked up at me just before he pulled the trigger on his drive at the first hole and said with a smile, "I'm going to do to this ball what I did to my girlfriend last night."

I took the bait and asked him, "What was that?"

He replied, "Drill it long and hard."

Whilst out on the golf course, two work colleagues were discussing the hot new secretary at their company.

Liam says, "I went back to her place last weekend and we had some great sex. She is better in bed than my wife."

Oliver said, "I went back to her place two days ago, and we had sex as well, but I still think your wife is better in bed."

A couple are playing in the annual Husband & Wife Club Championship. They are playing in a play-off hole and it is down to a 6 inch putt that the wife has to make.

Incredibly, she misses the putt and they lose the match.

On the way home in the car the husband is fuming, and he says to his wife, "I can't believe that you missed that putt. That putt was no longer than my willy."

The wife looked at her husband, smiled and said, "Yes dear, but it was much harder."

A very attractive woman arrived at a party. While scanning the guests, she spotted a man standing alone. She approached him, smiled and said, "Hello. My name is Carmen."

"That's a beautiful name," he replied. "Is it a family name?"

"No," she replied. "As a matter of fact I gave it to myself. It represents the things that I enjoy the most – cars and men. Therefore I chose 'Carmen.'"

"What's your name?" she asked.

He answered, "B. J. Titsengolf."

As a couple approaches the altar, the groom tells his wife-to-be, "Honey, I've got something to confess: I'm golf crazy, and every chance I get, I'll be playing golf."

"Since we're being honest," replies the bride, "I have to tell you that I'm a hooker."

The groom replies, "That's okay, honey. You just need to learn to keep your head down and your left arm straight."

Oliver got home from his Sunday round of golf later than normal, feeling very tired.

His wife asked, "Bad round, darling?"

Oliver replied, "Everything was going fine, then Terry has a heart attack and died on the 10th hole."

His wife said, "Oh, that's awful."

Oliver replied, "It sure was. For the whole back nine, it was hit the ball, drag Terry, hit the ball, drag Terry…"

A hacker hit a dreadful slice off the tee that ricocheted through the trees and onto an adjoining fairway, narrowly missing another golfer.

When he got to his ball, he was greeted by the unintentional target, who angrily told him of the near miss.

"I'm very sorry" the errant golfer said, "I didn't have time to shout fore."

"That's odd" the man replied," you had plenty of time to shout sh*t."

A recent study had some interesting conclusions on the weight of golfers at a well-known golf club.

This study indicated that single golfers are 'skinnier' than married ones.

The study's explanation for this result was interesting. It seems that the single golfer goes out and plays his round of golf, has a 'refreshment' at the 19th hole, goes home and goes to his refrigerator, finds nothing decent there and goes to bed.

The married golfer goes out and plays his round of golf, has a 'refreshment' at the 19th hole, goes home and goes to bed, finds nothing decent there, so he goes to his refrigerator.

When a woman wears a leather dress, a man's heart beats quicker, his throat gets dry and he goes weak at the knees, and he begins to think irrationally.

Ever wonder why?

It's probably because she smells like a new golf glove.

Three men are in a bar, bragging about their families.

The first guy says, "I have four sons. One more and I'll have a basketball team."

The second guy says, "That's nothing. I have ten sons. One more and I'll have a cricket team."

The third guy replies, "You guys haven't found true happiness. I have seventeen wives. One more and I'll have a golf course."

Two golfers are waiting their turn on the tee when a naked women runs across the course and into the woods.

Four men in white coats and another man carrying two buckets of sand are chasing her, and a little old man is bringing up the rear.

One of the golfers grabs the old man and asks," What's going on?"

The old man says, "She's a nymphomaniac from the asylum, she keeps escaping, and we are trying to catch her."

The golfer says, "What about the guy with the buckets of sand?"

The old man says, "That's his handicap. He caught her last time."

There was this guy who went golfing every Saturday and Sunday, it didn't matter what kind of weather – he played every weekend.

One Saturday he left the house early and headed for the golf course, but it was so bitterly cold that he decided he wouldn't golf that day and went back home.

His wife was still in bed when he got there, so he took off his clothes and snuggled up to her and said, "Terrible weather out there."

She replied, "Yeah, and can you believe my stupid husband went golfing."

A grandfather was at his grandson's wedding reception, giving him advice on having a happy marriage and a great life.

The young groom asked, "Grandfather, what's it like making love when you reach your age?"

The grandfather replied, "It's like putting with a rope."

Tom and Roy meet up on the golf course and decide to finish off the round together. Tom has a little dog with him and on the next green, when Tom holes out with a 30 foot putt, the little dog starts gently barking and stands up on its hind legs.

Roy is amazed at this clever trick and says, "That dog is really talented. What does it do if you miss a putt?"

Tom replies, "Somersaults."

Roy exclaims, "Wow - somersaults! How many does it do?"

Tom calmly replies, "It depends on how hard I kick it up the ass."

A hot shot lawyer sent gifts to some of his clients. The gifts were sleeves of golf balls, inscribed with the lawyer's name.

One of the recipients sent an email of thanks to the lawyer saying, "That's the first time I've ever had a lawyer buy the balls."

At a petrol station in rural Ireland, a Rolls Royce pulled up, driven by a well-dressed man in his golf attire. As he went to pay for his fuel, a couple of tees fell out of his pocket.

When the attendant asked what they were for, the golfer said, "They are for resting my balls on when I drive off."

The attendant sighed and said, "Rolls Royce really do think of everything."

A man got on a bus, with both of his trouser pockets full of golf balls, and sat down next to a beautiful blonde.

The blonde kept looking quizzically at him and his obviously bulging pants.

Finally, after a few glances from her, he said to her, "It's golf balls."

The blonde looked at him compassionately and said, "Oh you poor thing. I bet that hurts a lot more than tennis elbow."

Two couples were enjoying a competitive, best ball match, wives against husbands with the losers buying lunch and drinks.

On the final hole, the match was even and one of the wives had a long, breaking, fifteen foot putt to win the match. She lined the ball up carefully and confidently stroked the winning putt.

It was right on line, but unfortunately, it stopped three inches short of the hole.

Her husband thought that this was a riot and laughing said, "Right train, wrong ticket."

The wife failed to see the humor and not cracking a smile replied, "No sleeper cars on that train either."

One golfer says to another, "Your trouble is that you're not addressing the ball correctly."

The other golfer replies, "Maybe you're right. I've been too polite to the bloody thing for far too long."

Trevor was not having a good day at the golf course. After he missed a short putt, his partner asked him what the problem was.

"It's the wife," said Trevor. "As you know, she's taken up golf, and since she's been playing, she's cut my sex down to once a week."

"Well you should think yourself lucky," said his partner. "She's cut me out altogether."

Steve won first prize at a Father's Day tournament which was an envelope.

When he opened the envelope, he was very surprised to find a voucher for a free visit to a brothel. He had never been to one before but he decided to go the next day even though he was very nervous.

The girls were very friendly and he soon found a young lady he fancied and he went with her to her room.

Ten minutes later, she came running back to the Madam and asked, "Can you tell me what a Mulligan is?"

I played today with a married couple who were in their mid 60's. She used to b e a teacher and said that she never swore because she didn't want to slip up in the class room.

She duffed a chip shot on the second hole and said, "Ain't that a tutti frutti?"

Puzzled, I looked over to her husband who translated for me by saying, "Ain't that a mother f*cker?"

Three lady golfers are on the tee talking about their husbands.

The first lady says, "My husband is like a Ferrari. He is a fantastic performer."

The second lady says, "My husband is like a Tesla. He is smooth, silent and knows what to do."

The third lady says, "My husband is like an old banger. He only manages to get going once a year, and even then he has to be started by hand."

Two couples went out golfing together.

The men hit first from the men's tee and walked with the ladies to their tee box.

The first lady took a mighty swing at the ball, missing it completely, while passing some gas rather loudly in the process.

No one commented.

She addressed the ball again but this time she passed just a little gas as she made contact with the ball, topping it and moving it a short distance.

She said, "I wonder why it didn't go any further."

One of the men said, "I don't think you gave it enough gas."

Two women golfers come to a par 3.

The first woman hits her shot straight and the ball finishes in the middle of the green.

The second woman takes a solid swing and leaves her ball one centimeter from the first ball.

The other woman says, "Wow. I've never seen two balls so close before."

A murder has been committed and the police had been called to an apartment where they found a man holding a 9 iron in his hand, looking at the lifeless body of a woman on the floor.

The detective asks, "Sir, is that your wife?"

The guy replies, "Yes."

The detective asks, "Did you hit her with that golf club?"

The guy replies, "Yes, yes I did."

The man stifles a sob, drops the club and puts his hands on his head.

The detective asks, "How many times did you hit her?"

The guy replies, "I'm not sure. Five, six, seven? Put me down for a five."

A guy comes home from work and is greeted by his wife dressed in a sexy little nightie.

"Tie me up," she purrs, "and you can do anything you want."

So he ties her up and goes out for a round of golf.

A beggar is shuffling along the street when he asks a man for 10 dollars.

"Will you buy booze with it?" the man asks.

The beggar replies, "No."

"Will you gamble the money?" the man asks.

The beggar replies, "No."

"Will you make bets at the golf course?" the man asks.

The beggar replies, "No, I don't play golf."

The man then says, "I want you to come home with me so my wife can see what happens to a man who doesn't drink, gamble or play golf."

Two slutty blondes are passing by the half-open door to the men's changing rooms at the golf club when they notice a man who has his face obscured by the towel he is using to dry his hair.

However, they do get a good view of his body from the waist down.

One of the blondes says to the other, "Well, I didn't see his face, but he's certainly not my husband."

The other blonde replies, "I had a very good look, and I don't recognize him - he must be a new member."

Tickets for the Masters are notoriously expensive, and the scalpers and touts make lots of money during the week of the tournament.

One of my buddies was offered a day's ticket to last year's tournament for 1,500 dollars.

My friend said, "That's absurd. I could get a woman for that."

The tout replied, "That's true sir, but with this ticket you get eighteen holes."

Paul and Robert were playing in Florida.

Paul putted out at the seventh green and walked back to the cart. As Robert sank his putt, Paul suddenly jumped up out of the cart and dropped his pants. He had just sat on a bee and got a nasty sting and he desperately asked his partner to get the stinger out.

The sight of a man kneeling next to his playing partner's bare rear end was just too much for the group playing behind them.

The group raced up to Paul and Robert and asked, "Just what was the bet?"

A guy goes to a new golf club and in the pro shop a very tasty woman smiles and says, "Hello there."

He is rather taken aback, and although she looks familiar he can't place where he might know her from, so he says "Sorry, do you know me?"

She replies, "I think you might be the father of one of my kids."

His mind shoots back to the one and only time he has been unfaithful to his wife.

"Christ." he says "are you the stripper from my stag night that I shagged on the putting green and then later you whipped me with some wet celery and stuck a cucumber up my @rse?"

"No" she replies, "I'm your son's English teacher."

One day this woman went to her local golf pro, and told him she had developed a huge slice.

Day and night he worked with her for three months.

Now she's the biggest hooker in town.

Sam's wife is at home in bed with her husband's best friend Mark.

After making love, the phone rings and Sam's wife answers it.

Mark hears just her side of the conversation.

"Hello darling, How are you? Really, that's great. I'm so pleased for you. That sounds like you're doing well. Great. Thanks. See you later. Love you too."

She hangs up the phone and Mark asks her, "Who was that?"

"Oh," she replies, "that was Sam telling me all about the great time he's having on the golf course with you."

My golfing buddy Francis saw a fortune teller the other day, who told him he would come into some money.

The following weekend he f*cked a girl called Penny, so the fortune teller got it right.

A husband and wife had a huge disagreement and in an attempt to kiss and make up, she went to the pro shop to buy him a gift.

She asked, "How much is this fancy new spider putter?"

The pro replied, "350 dollars."

She said, "I want to make it special for him to make up with him after our major argument."

The pro said, "May I suggest you also have it engraved?"

"What shall I say?" she asked.

The pro replied, "What about, 'Never Up, Never In?'"

"Oh no." she gasped. "That's what the argument was about."

On the wall in in the men's toilet at the golf club is some graffiti that says, 'My wife follows me everywhere.'

Written underneath it is, 'No, I don't'

An Oriental businessman was out of the country on a business trip.

He was taken out for a round of golf, although he had never played golf before.

When he got home, his family asked him how the trip had gone.

The man replied, "I played interesting game. Hit little white ball with long stick in large cow pasture."

They asked him what the name of the game was.

He replied, "Name of game is 'Oh Shit'"

Simon is in the clubhouse bar thinking about his mistress.

Deep in thought, he absent-mindedly starts thinking aloud.

"It's not worth it," he mutters, "it's never as good as you hoped. It's expensive and it drives my wife mad."

A pal overheard Simon's words and leaned across to him and said, "Come on, Simon, you knew what to expect when you took up golf."

Lee and Marvin were on the third tee waiting for the group in front to clear.

Marvin says to Lee, "I just let out a silent fart. What do you think I should do?"

Marvin replied, "Put a new battery in your hearing aid."

Remember, you can easily tweak most of these gags for your own storytelling purpose, so in this example, you would say something like this.

I was playing golf with Marvin yesterday.

On the third tee he said to me, "I just let out a silent fart. What do you think I should do?"

I told him to put a new battery in his hearing aid.

Three buddies are in the clubhouse bar discussing the relative merits of having a wife or mistress.

Andrew says, "It's better to have a wife because the sense of security lowers your stress levels, and is good for your health."

Bruce says, "It's better to have a mistress. It's much more exciting and invigorating, and she will be more adventurous."

Charles says, "You're both wrong. It's best to have both so that when the wife thinks you're with the mistress and the mistress thinks you're with the wife, you can go and play a round of golf."

Chapter 6: Longer Rude Golfer Jokes

Remember, that the names used in this book are the products of the author's imagination or used in a fictitious manner. Any resemblance to actual persons, living or dead is purely coincidental. Of course, you can easily change any of the names to suit your own story telling purposes.

What's In A Lie

Roger, a 70 year-old, extremely wealthy widower, shows up at the country club with a breathtakingly beautiful and very sexy 25 year-old blonde.

She hangs onto Roger's arm and listens intently to his every word.

His buddies at the club are all aghast.

At the very first chance, they corner him and ask, "How did you get the trophy girlfriend?"

Roger replies, "Girlfriend? She's my trophy wife."

They're amazed, but ask, "So, how did you persuade her to marry you?"

Roger replies, "I lied about my age."

The pals ask, "Did you tell her you were only 50?"

Roger smiles and says, "No, I told her I was 90."

The Provisional Ball

A married couple played golf together everyday.

One day the man and his wife were on the first tee of their local course. He was on the white tee and she was waiting in front of him by the ladies tee.

He teed off and caught the ball cleanly; but unfortunately, it hit his wife smack in the back of the head killing her instantly.

There was an inquest on the wife's death, and the coroner said it was clear how she died, in that she was killed by a golf ball, and that there was a perfect imprint of a Titleist 1 golf ball on the back of her head.

The husband said, "Yes, that was my ball."

The coroner then went on to say that he was a bit concerned to find a Titleist 3 ball inserted up the woman's backside, and could the husband throw some light on this?

The husband said, "Oh that must have been my provisional. I wondered where that ball went."

The Leprechaun

One fine day in Ireland, a guy is out golfing and on the 12th hole he slices his drive into the woods on the side of the fairway.

He goes looking for his ball and comes across this little guy lying on the ground with a huge lump on his head, and the golf ball right beside him.

"Goodness," says the golfer, and proceeds to revive the poor little guy.

Upon awaking, the little guy says, "Well, you caught me fair and square. I am a leprechaun and I will grant you three wishes."

The golfer says, "I can't take anything from you, I'm just glad I didn't hurt you too badly," and walks away.

Watching the golfer depart, the leprechaun thinks, "Well, he was a nice enough guy, and he did catch me, so I have to do something for him. I'll give him the three things that I would want. I'll give him unlimited money, a great golf game, and a great sex life."

Well, a year later the same golfer hits one into the same woods on the same hole and goes off looking for his ball.

When he finds the ball he sees the same leprechaun and asks how he is doing. The leprechaun says, "I'm fine, and might I ask how your golf game is?"

The golfer says, "It's incredible these days. I play to par every time."

The leprechaun says, "I did that for you. And might I ask how your money is holding out?"

The golfer says, "Well, now that you mention it, every time I put my hand in my pocket, I pull out a ten Euros note."

The leprechaun smiles and says, "I did that for you. And might I ask how your sex life is?"

The golfer looks at him a little shyly and says, "Well, maybe once or twice a week."

The leprechaun stammers, "Once or twice a week?"

The golfer, a little embarrassed, looks at him and says, "Well, that's not too bad for a Catholic priest in a small parish."

The Hospital Visit

A man staggered into a hospital with concussion, multiple bruises, a black eye, and a five iron wrapped tightly around his throat.

The doctor asked him, "What happened to you?"

The bruised guy replied, "Well, I was playing a round of golf with my wife, when at a difficult hole, she sliced her ball into a cow pasture. We went to look for it and while I was looking around I noticed one of the cows had something white at its rear end."

He continued, "I walked over, lifted its tail, and sure enough, there was a golf ball with my wife's monogram on it - stuck right in the middle of the cow's butt."

"I held the cow's tail up and I yelled to my wife, 'Hey Honey, this looks like yours.'"

"I don't remember much after that."

Gotcha

Ronnie was a 9 handicapper, and one day he challenged the pro to a match off scratch. He proposed they put up $100 each on the outcome.

"But," Ronnie said to the pro, "since you're so much better than me, you have to give me three 'gotchas'."

"A 'gotcha'?" the golf pro asked, "what's that?"

"Don't worry," Ronnie replied, "I'll use one of my 'gotchas' on the first tee and you'll understand."

The golf pro figured that whatever 'gotchas' were, giving up only three of them was no big deal - especially if one had to be used on the first tee. So he agreed to the bet, and the pro and Ronnie headed to the first tee to start their match.

Later in the bar, club members were amazed to see the pro handing Ronnie $100. The pro had lost to Ronnie and they asked the pro what happened.

"Well," the pro said, "I took the club back on the first tee, and as I started my downswing, Ronnie knelt behind me, reached up between my legs and grabbed my crotch, and yelled 'Gotcha.'"

Slow Play

Graham and his partner Harry are being held up by two women who are playing terribly slowly.

Finally, after watching the women in the distance as they stood over their putts for what seemed like an eternity, Graham decided to do something.

He said, "I'll walk ahead and ask them if we can play through."

He set off down the fairway, walking towards the women. But when he got halfway, he stopped, turned around and headed back to where Harry was waiting.

"I can't do it," Graham said, sounding embarrassed. "One of them is my wife and the other is my mistress."

"OK," Harry said, "Then I'll go ask them."

Harry started up the fairway, only to stop halfway and turn back.

"What's wrong?" Graham asked.

Harry replied, "Small world, isn't it?"

Bi-Focals

Nigel is waiting to tee off for the start of his round when he sees Roy just finishing his round.

Nigel notices that Roy is wet all over the front of his trousers. Curiosity gets the best of him, so he asks Roy how he got so wet.

Roy said, "Today was the first time I have played with bifocals. All day long, I could see two sizes for everything. There was a big club and a little club; a big ball and a little ball and so on."

Roy continued, "I hit the little ball with the big club and it went straight and long all day long. On the green, I putted the little ball into the big hole. I played some of the best golf of my life."

Nigel said, "That's very interesting, but how did you get all wet?"

"Well," said Roy, "when I got to the 16th, I needed to urinate. I went into the woods and unzipped my fly. When I looked down, there were two of them; a big one and a little one. Well, I knew the big one wasn't mine, so I put it back in my pants."

Struck By Lightning

Michael was out golfing one day and was unfortunately struck by lightning.

At the Pearly Gates, Saint Peter told him that the bolt of lightning was actually meant for his golfing partner, but as God doesn't want it known that he makes mistakes; he would have to go back to Earth as someone other than himself.

Michael thought about if for a while and told Saint Peter that he would like to go back to earth as a lesbian.

Saint Peter asked why a macho guy like him would want to back to Earth as a lesbian.

Michael replied, "It's simple really. That way, I can still get to make love to a woman AND I can play from the red tees."

Afterlife Vow

Many years ago Jason and Rebecca made a vow that whoever dies first will come back to inform the other of the afterlife.

A year after Jason died, true to his word, he makes contact.

"Rebecca... Rebecca," he says, "can you hear me?"

"Is that you, Jason?" asks Rebecca.

"Yes, my dear," he replies, "I've come back, just as we agreed."

"So what is it like?" asks Rebecca.

Jason replies, "Well, every morning I wake up and have sex. I have breakfast and then I go to the golf course where I have sex. I run around, sunbathe sometimes, and after lunch I have more sex. In the afternoon I romp around the golf course, then have more sex. It's like this very day."

"Oh, Jason," says Rebecca, "you really must be in Heaven."

"Not exactly, darling," replies Jason, "I've come back as a rabbit on Royal Birkdale golf course."

Double Trouble

This guy had just completed a rough divorce and decided that he would like to go out and play a relaxing round of golf.

While waiting on the first tee, he reached into the trash can and pulled out a rusty lamp. He rubbed it to get the dirt off and a genie popped out. The genie told the guy that he would grant him three wishes, under the condition that his ex-wife would get double what he wished for.

The guy said he wanted a Ferrari. The genie reminded him that his ex-wife would get two of them. The guy had no hesitation and said he didn't care if his ex-wife had two, as long as he had one for himself. Poof! The genie said it was done.

The guy's next wish was $1 million in the back of his Ferrari. The genie reminded him that his ex-wife would receive $2 million. The guy said he didn't care and told the genie to fulfill his wish. Poof! The genie said it was done.

The guy thought long and hard before deciding on his final wish. Eventually, he handed the genie his 6-iron and said calmly, "Beat me half to death."

Hung Lo

Three guys are on the first tee waiting for the fourth guy – a certain Mr Hung Lo. His boss is one of the four ball group that is waiting for him, so he calls Hung and asks, "Why you late Hung?"

Hung replies, "Hey boss, I not come golf today. I sick. I got headache. I got earache. I not come golf."

His boss says, "Hung, I really need you today. You're the best golfer at my company. I will re-arrange the match for 2pm this afternoon."

The boss continued, "When I feel sick I go to my wife and tell her give me sex. It make everything better and I can go play golf. You try."

At 1:30pm, there is no sign of Hung, so his boss gets on his mobile and calls Hung to ask where he is,

Hung replies, "I am on my way. I do what you say and I now feel great. I be at golf soon. You got nice house, boss."

The Golf Tour

Trevor and his buddies were talking about planning a week long golf tour.

He had to tell them that unfortunately he couldn't go because his wife wouldn't let him.

After a lot of teasing and name calling, Trevor headed home totally frustrated.

The following week when Trevor's buddies arrived at the golf resort, they were shocked to see Trevor sitting in the lobby, drinking a beer, with his golf clubs next to him.

They asked, "How did you talk your wife into letting you go, Trevor?"

"I didn't have to," Trevor replied.

He continued, "Last night I was slumped down in my chair with a beer. Then, my wife sneaked up behind me, covered my eyes and said, 'Surprise.' When I peeled her hands back, she was standing there in a beautiful see-through negligee and said, "Carry me into the bedroom and tie me to the bed, and you can do whatever you want."

"So here I am!"

An Expensive Quickie

A boss and his sexy secretary are playing golf and every time she addresses the ball, she shows off her shapely ass, which gives her boss the horn.

On the 15th tee, on a part of the course that is secluded, the boss simply can't take it any longer.

He says, "I really want to have sex with you. I promise I will be very fast and I'll make it worth your while. I'll throw 1,000 dollars down into those bushes and by the time you bend down to pick it all up, I'll be done."

The secretary pondered for a moment then decided to call her boyfriend who told her, "Do it. Just make sure you pick up the money really quickly - he won't have time to undress himself."

Half an hour passes and the boyfriend calls his girlfriend to find out what happened.

She says, trying to catch her breath, "The bastard used coins. I'm still picking, and he's still f*cking."

A Hole Behind

While playing on the front nine of a golf course with an odd layout, this male golfer was confused as to where he was on the course.

Looking around, he saw a lady golfer and he asked her if she knew what hole he was playing.

She replied, "I'm on the 8th hole, and you are a hole behind me, so you must be on the 7th hole."

On the back nine the same thing happened; and he approached her again with the same request.

She replied, "I'm on the 13th hole, and you are a hole behind me, so you must be on the 12th hole."

After he had finished his round he was having a drink, when he saw the same lady sitting in one of the comfy seats on her own.

He asked the barman if he knew her and he said that she was a sales lady who played the course regularly.

The golfer approached her and said, "Let me buy you a drink to thank for your help today. I understand that you are in the sales profession. I'm also in sales. What do you sell?"

She replied, "If I tell you, I bet you'll laugh."

He said, "No, I won't."

"Well, if you must know," she answered, "I work for Tampax."

Hearing that, he laughed out loud.

She said, "See I told you that you would laugh."

"That's not what I'm laughing at," he replied. "I'm a salesman for Preparation H, so I'm still a hole behind you."

The Honeymooners

A guy is out on the golf course when he takes a high speed ball right in the crotch.

Writhing in agony, he falls to the ground.

As soon as he could manage, he took himself to the doctor and said, "How bad is it doc? I'm going on my honeymoon next week and my fiancée is still a virgin."

The doctor told him, "I'll have to put your penis in a splint to let it heal and keep it straight. It should be okay within a week."

So the doctor busily got to work. He took four bondage style tongue depressors and shaped an immaculate four sided bandage, and wired it all together; it was an extraordinary work of art when he had finished.

The guy decides not to mention any of this to his fiancée.

A week later, on their wedding night in the hotel room she peels open her blouse to reveal a gorgeous set of breasts.

She says to her new husband, "You're the first; no one has ever touched these breasts."

He immediately drops his trousers and replies, "Look at this, it's still in the crate!"

Adios Angelo

The country club announced in their newsletter that the senior caddie Angelo was leaving the club.

During his last week, one lady member invited him to have lunch at her house overlooking the course.

After lunch, the lady invited him up to the bedroom for some dessert which he gladly accepted.

After some ravishing sex, the lady member handed Angelo a dollar.

Confused, Angelo asked, "What's the dollar for?"

The lady replied, "It was my husband's suggestion. When I told him you were leaving and asked him if we should get you something for all the years you worked at the club, he told me, 'Fuck him, give him a dollar.'"

Ambidextrous

A couple of weeks ago, I played with a new member who shot an even par 72.

We had fun during the round, so I asked him if he wanted to play next week.

He said, "Sure, but I might be half an hour late."

The following week he shows up right on time, and sets up on the first tee this time playing left-handed; and again he shoots a 72.

I asked him if he wanted to play again next week.

He replied, "Sure but I might be half an hour late."

I then asked him, "How come sometimes you play right-handed and other times you play left-handed."

He said, "When I wake up in the morning and my wife is sleeping on her left side, I play left-handed and if she is on her right side, then I play right-handed."

I then asked, "So, what if she is lying flat on her back?"

He replied, "That's when I'll be half an hour late."

The Lion Tamer

A circus owner runs an ad for an amateur lion tamer and two people showed up.

He's a retired golfer in his late fifties and she is a gorgeous babe in her mid-twenties.

The circus owner tells them, "Be careful in there - this is one ferocious lion. He ate my last tamer so you had better be good or you're likely to be lunch too."

The hot girl says, "I'll go first."

She walks past the chair and the whip and steps right into the lion's cage. The lion starts to snarl and pant and begins to charge her. About halfway there, she throws open her coat revealing her beautiful naked body.

The lion stops dead in his tracks, sheepishly crawls up to her and starts licking her feet and ankles. He continues to lick her entire body for several minutes and then rests his head at her feet.

The circus owner's jaw is on the floor. He says, "I've never seen a display like that in my life."

He then turns to the golfer and asks, "Can you do that?"

The old golfer replies without hesitation, "No problem, just get that lion out of there first."

Fancy Watch

A gorgeous young lady was beginning a round by herself one evening when the golf pro asked to join her.

She agreed and said, "Sure, I might get some golf tips from you as well if you don't mind."

After a few holes, she asked the assistant pro about the gadget on his wrist and asked if it was a distance measuring GPS device.

The pro replied, "No, it's a very fancy watch."

The lady said, "But it has a blank face, how can you tell the time?"

The pro said, "Oh, it's one of those new telepathic psychic watches which transmits the time to me telepathically."

The gorgeous woman asked, "Woah, what do you mean?"

The pro looked at his watch; studied it for a few seconds, and then said, "Well it tells me you're not wearing any knickers."

She smiled assuredly and said, "You're wrong, I am wearing knickers."

The pro looked at his watch again, shook his wrist, cleaned the watch face, shook it again, then looked at it and said, "Oh, it's running about an hour fast."

Marriage Guidance

A husband and wife go to a marriage guidance counselor as their marriage is having major difficulties.

The counselor asks them what the problem is and the wife went into a rant, listing every problem they have ever had in the fifteen years they've been married, including neglect, lack of respect, lack of intimacy, feeling empty and lonely.

It turned into a long list of unmet needs she felt she had endured over the course of their marriage.

After allowing this to go on for quite a long time, the counselor puts his pen down, stands up, walks around the desk, and embraced the woman, kissing her passionately while cuddling her.

The woman then quietly sits down in a daze.

The counselor turns to the husband and says, "That is what your wife needs at least three times a week, can you manage that?"

The husband thought for a moment and replied, "No I can't. I play golf on Mondays and Fridays, but I can bring her in on Wednesdays."

The Masseuse

Two women were playing golf. One teed off and watched in horror as her ball headed directly toward a group of men playing the next hole. The ball hit one of the men. He immediately clasped his hands together at his groin, fell to the ground and rolled around in agony.

The woman rushed up, and apologized.

She said, "Please let me help. I'm a physical therapist and I know I could relieve your pain if you'd allow me."

"Oh, no, I'll be all right. I'll be fine in a few minutes," the man replied.

It was obvious that he was in agony, lying in the fetal position, still clasping his hands together at his groin.

The female golfer urged him to let him help him, so at her persistence, he allowed her to help.

She gently took his hands away and laid them to his side, loosened his trousers and put her hands inside. She administered tender and artful gentle massage to his privates.

Five minutes later the man was sighing with satisfaction when she asked, "How does that feel?"

He replied, "That feels great, but I think it's my right-hand thumb that really hurts."

The Sex Toy

Two golfers were in the bar after a round when Oliver says, "My wife has a lot of nerve being angry with me."

Andy says, "You mean she won't let you out to play golf?"

Oliver replies, "No, that's not it. I insist on making love in the dark, and have done for over 20 years. Anyway last night, she turns on the light and finds me holding a vibrator."

He continues, "She says 'You impotent sod, how could you lie to me for all these years?'"

Andy says, "Are you really impotent?"

Oliver replies, "Yes I am, but so what?"

Andy says, "Well she should be angry. What did you say to her?"

Oliver replies, "I looked her straight in the eye and calmly said, I'll explain the sex toy, you explain the kids."

Sixty Nine

A good young golfer playing in a local tournament was being followed around by an older woman who had the hots for him.

After he had finished with a round of 69 she went up to him and told him how much she had enjoyed watching him play and she invited him to dinner and the young guy gratefully accepted.

At dinner that night, she was dressed provocatively and she said, "It was great to watch a young handsome man like you play. You've got great possibilities ahead of you."

The young guy politely replied, "Thanks. I don't shoot a 69 very often."

The horny woman winked and said, "How about you and I have a 69 together?"

The inexperienced young guy said, "What's a 69?"

The woman seductively said, "Well, you put your head between my legs, and I put my head between your legs."

The young guy smiled as the older woman slowly undressed.

As he put his head between her legs, she let out a roaring fart.

She sniggered, "Oh I'm so sorry, please excuse me."

The young guy nodded then put his head between her legs when she let out another deafening fart right in his face.

"Oops, sorry again." she said.

The young golfer stood up, put this clothes on, and while walking out exclaimed, "I'm not doing that another 67 times."

12 Inch BIC

Two guys were playing golf when one pulled out a cigar but he didn't have a lighter, so he asked his partner if he had one.

"I sure do," he replied, and he reached into his golf bag and pulled out a 12-inch BIC lighter.

His pal exclaimed, "Where did you get that from?"

"I got it from my genie." said the first guy.

"You have a genie?" his friend asked.

"Yep, he's in my golf bag." He opens up his golf bag and out pops a genie.

The friend says to the genie, "I'm a good friend of your master, will you grant me a wish?"

The genie replies, "Yes, I will."

The friend asks the genie for 'a million bucks.'

The genie replies, "It will be done."

He hops back into the golf bag and leaves the golfers standing there waiting for the 'million bucks.'

Suddenly the sky darkens and soon a million ducks surround the golfers.

"Hey," yells the disappointed golfer. "I asked your genie for a million bucks, not a million ducks."

"Sorry," the other golfer replied, "He's hard of hearing, and besides, do you really think that I'd ask a genie for a 12-inch BIC?"

Promises, Promises

Four married guys were golfing. While playing the 4th hole, the following conversation took place:

Chris says, "You have no idea what I had to do to be able to come out golfing this weekend. I had to promise my wife that I will paint the spare room next weekend."

Derek says, "That's nothing, I had to promise my wife I will build a patio."

Bryan says, "Man, you both have it easy! I had to promise my wife I will re-do the kitchen for her."

They continued to play the hole when they realized that Nigel hadn't said anything.

So they asked him, "You haven't said anything about what you had to do to be able to come golfing this weekend. What's the deal?"

Nigel says, "You were lucky. I set my alarm for 6:30 a.m. and when it went off, I gave the wife a gentle nudge and said, 'golf course or intercourse?'"

She said, "Wear your sweater."

Cheating Wife

Peter and Julie are celebrating their 50th wedding anniversary.

Peter asks his wife, "Julie, I was wondering, have you ever cheated on me?"

Julie replies, "Oh Peter, why would you ask such a question now? You don't want to know the answer to that question."

Peter says, "Yes, Julie, I really want to know. Please."

Julie replies, "Well, all right darling, if you insist. Yes, I have cheated on you three times."

Peter says, "Three? When were they?"

Julie replies, "Well, remember when you were 30 years old and you really wanted to start your own business and no bank would give you a loan? Remember, then one day the bank manager came over to the house and signed the loan papers?"

Peter says, "Oh, Julie, you did that for me. I respect you even more than ever, to do such a thing for me. So, when was number 2?"

Julie replies, "Well, remember a few years ago when you were really ill and you were in need of that operation, and the waiting list was months? Then remember how Dr. Harris came all the way out here, and then you got booked in the following week?"

Peter says, "I can't believe that you would do such a thing for me, to save my life. I couldn't have a more wonderful wife than you Julie. To do such a thing, you must really love me. So, when was number 3?"

Julie replies, "Well, remember a few years ago, when you really wanted to be captain of the golf club and you were nine votes short?"

The Mermaid

A Frenchman, an Italian and a Scotsman were playing golf on a links course when they spotted a stunning sexy mermaid on the beach.

They all dropped their clubs and ran down to get a closer look.

The mermaid was incredibly beautiful and voluptuous.

The Frenchman, burning with desire, said, "Have you ever been kissed?" "No, I haven't," answered the mermaid. So the Frenchman walked over and kissed her long and hard.

"Hmmm," sighed the mermaid, "that's good."

The Italian, not to be outdone, asked the mermaid, "Have you ever been fondled?" "No, I haven't," whispered the mermaid. So the Italian walked over and spent some time fondling her breasts.

"Hmmm," sighed the mermaid, "that's good."

Finally the Scotsman asked her, "Have you ever been f*cked?" "No, I haven't," answered the mermaid. "Well, you have now," said the Scotsman, "'because the tide's out!"

Girls Night Out

Two women had gone for a girls' night out.

Both were very faithful and loving wives, but they did like a drink, and in particular the happy hour wine deals.

This particular night, they were exceptionally drunk and on their walk home they desperately needed to wee, so they stopped in the local cemetery.

One of them had nothing to wipe with so she decided to take off her panties and use them.

Her friend however was wearing rather expensive panties and she did not want to soil them.

She squatted down next to a grave that had a wreath with a ribbon on it, so she proceeded to wipe herself with that.

After the girls had done their business, they stumbled their way home.

The next morning, the husband of one of the women phoned the other husband and said, "These girls nights out have got to stop. I'm beginning to suspect the worst. My wife came home last night with no panties."

"That's nothing," said the other husband, "mine came back with a card stuck to her @rse that said, "From all the guys at the golf club. We'll never forget you."

Deserted

A hacker had treated himself to playing the Emirates golf club in Dubai where he met a very beautiful virgin woman. They got talking and he persuaded her to come with him into the desert to find an oasis and escape the crowds.

The guy hired a camel, provisions for a few days, and they set off across the desert. After a few hours, the camel, suffering from exhaustion after carrying the pair of them, keeled over and died.

The woman dusted herself down and said, "This looks grim. I am not sure how long we will able to surve out here in this heat."

The guy said, "You mean I won't be able to ever play golf again. That really is grim."

He then said, "Since we are unable to make it out of here alive, would you do something for me?"

She replied, "What do you have in mind?"

He said, "I have never seen a virgin woman's breasts before and I wondered if I might see yours."

She said, "Under the circumstances, I can't see any harm in that" and she then opened her gown to show a pair of exquisitely formed breasts.

The guy said, "They're truly divine, May I touch them?"

She blushed but consented and he fondled them for several minutes.

The young virgin spoke, "Could I ask something of you? Only I have never seen a man's penis and under the circumstances, do you think I could see yours?"

The guys thought for a second, said OK and took his trousers off.

She asked, "May I touch it?"

He replied, "Oh yeah."

After a few minutes fondling, the guy had a huge erection.

He whispered, "Do you know that if I insert my penis in the right place, it can give life."

She then declared, "Then why don't you stick your dick up that camel's arse, and let's get the hell out of here."

The Fairy

A man was playing a round on his own, and on the 15th hole he hooked his ball into some buttercups along the left of the fairway.

Being an honorable man, he penalized himself one stroke and moved his ball out of the pretty flowers.

A fairy then appeared and she said, "Thank you for moving your ball out of the earth's beautiful buttercups, you will now be blessed with an unlimited supply of butter for the rest of your life."

"Well, thanks," the man replied, "but where were you yesterday when I hit my ball into the pussywillows?

You can re-work this gag, as follows.

I played the Berkshire the other day. On the 15th I hooked my drive into some buttercups.

I didn't want to damage the little plants, so I took a drop and after I played my next shot, a fairy appeared.

She said, "Thank you for not damaging the buttercups. As your reward, you will now be blessed with an unlimited supply of butter for the rest of your life."

I said, "Thanks, but where were you on the previous hole when I hit my ball into the pussywillows?"

Dammit – I Missed

A priest and an atheist are playing golf together.

On the first hole, the atheist misses a short putt, and exclaims, "Dammit, I missed."

The priest says, "Do not use the Lord's name in vain, or he may punish you."

On the second hole, the atheist tries a particularly aggressive chip shot to get the ball onto the green and instead lands in a bunker. "Dammit, I missed." exclaimed the atheist, to which the priest again issued a warning about God punishing those who curse.

The round continues in much the same way, with the atheist continuing to exclaim "Dammit I missed." every time he hits an errant ball and the priest continues to admonish him about God's wrath.

Finally, they get to the eighteenth hole and the score is tied. The atheist needs to make a two-foot putt in order to win. He taps the ball, and again he misses, and again, he says, "Dammit, I missed."

Before the priest can respond the clouds in the sky open up, and a bolt of lightning shoots out and hits the priest, killing him.

From the clouds above a deep voice says, "Dammit, I missed."

The Hit Man

Two old friends were just about to tee off at the first hole of their local golf course when a guy asked, "Do you mind if I join you? My partner didn't turn up."

"Sure," they said, "You're welcome."

So they started playing and enjoyed the game and the company of the newcomer. Part way around the course, one of the friends asked the newcomer, "What do you do for a living?"

"I'm a hit man," was the reply.

"You're kidding." was the response.

"No, I'm not," he said, reaching into his golf bag, and pulling out a sniper's rifle with a large telescopic sight.

"That's amazing," said the other friend, "Can I take a look through the telescopic sight? I think I might be able to see my house from here."

So he picked up the rifle and looked through the sight in the direction of his house.

He said, "Yeah, I can see my house all right. This sight is fantastic. I can see right in the window. Wow, I can see my wife in the bedroom. Yikes, I can see she's naked. Hang on a minute, that's my neighbor in there with her and wait a second, he's naked, too."

He turned to the hit man, "How much do you charge for a hit?"

The hit man replied, "I'll do a flat rate, for you, one thousand dollars every time I pull the trigger."

The guy asked, "Can you do two for me now?"

The hit man replied, "Sure, what do you want?"

The guy said, "First, shoot my wife; she's always been a mouthy cow, so shoot her in the mouth. Then the neighbor, he's a friend of mine, so just shoot his dick off to teach him a lesson."

The hit man picked up the rifle and took aim, standing perfectly still for a few minutes.

"Are you going to do it or not?" said the golfer impatiently.

"Just be patient," said the hit man calmly, "I think I can save you a grand here."

The Affair

A married man was having an affair with his secretary. One day, their passions overcame them and they went to her house for some afternoon delight.

Exhausted from the afternoon's activities, they fell asleep and awoke at around 7p.m.

As the man put on his clothes, he told his secretary to take his shoes outside and rub them through the grass and dirt.

Mystified, she nonetheless complied and he slipped into his shoes and drove home.

When he entered the house, his wife asked, "Where have you been?"

"Darling," replied the man, "I can't lie to you. I've been having an affair with my secretary. I fell asleep in her bed and didn't wake up until seven o'clock."

The wife glanced down at his shoes and said, "You liar. You've been out playing golf."

Ship High In Transit

In the 17th century, most products were transported by ship and it was also before the invention of commercial fertilizer, so large shipments of manure were common.

It was shipped dry, because it weighed less but once water hit it, fermentation began which produced methane gas as a by-product.

The manure was stored in bundles below deck and once wet with sea water, methane began to build up.

If someone came below decks at night with a lantern, then Boom, there would often be a huge explosion.

Several ships were destroyed in this manner before the cause of the explosions was determined.

Afterwards, the bundles of manure were stamped with the term "Ship High In Transit" which directed the crew to stow it in the upper decks so that any water that came into the hold would not reach this volatile cargo and produce the explosive gas.

Thus evolved the term "S.H.I.T" (**S**hip **H**igh **I**n **T**ransit) which has come down through the centuries and is still in use today.

You probably didn't know the history of this word.

Neither did I. I always thought it was a golf term.

Hole In One

Paul had been playing for twenty years but never had a hole-in-one.

As he was hacking away in a bunker he voiced the thought, "I'd give anything to get a hole-in-one."

"Anything?" came a voice from behind. Paul turned around to see a small grinning, red-clad figure with horns and a tail.

"Would you give up half your sex life?" asked the devilish figure.

"Yes, Yes I would." Paul instantly replied.

"It's a deal then." said the horned figure who then disappeared.

On the very next hole Paul's tee shot looked good the moment he hit it, with the ball flying into the hole for his first ever hole-in-one.

At the end of the round, the figure in red appeared again.

"Now for our bargain," he said. "You remember you must give up half your sex life."

Paul grimaced, "That gives me a bit of a problem."

"Don't try and back out of this," cried the figure. "We struck a bargain and you agreed to it."

Paul replied, "Yes, of course. But I have a problem. Which half of my sex life do you want - the thinking or the dreaming?"

Behind A Tree

Two English guys were playing golf when the first one said, "I really need to take a crap."

The second replied, "Well go behind that tree and do your stuff."

The first guy looks over at the tree and says, "But I don't have any toilet paper."

The second man remarks, "You have five pounds on you, don't you? Use that to wipe yourself."

Reluctantly, the first guy goes and does his stuff.

Minutes later he comes back with crap all over him.

The second guy asks, "What happened? Didn't you use the five pounds?"

The first guy replies, "Yes, but have you ever tried to wipe your arse with four pound coins and two 50 pences?"

The Ducks

Three golfing buddies died in a car crash and went to heaven.

Upon arrival, they saw the most beautiful golf course they have ever seen. St. Peter told them they were welcome to play the course, but he cautioned them, "Don't step on the ducks."

The men had blank expressions on their faces, and one of them said, "The ducks?"

"Yes," St. Peter said. "There are millions of ducks walking around the golf course, and when one of them is stepped on, he squawks, and then the one next to him squawks, and soon they're all making a dreadful racket, and it really breaks the tranquility. If you step on the ducks, you'll be severely punished."

The men start playing the course, and within 20 minutes, one of the guys stepped on a duck. The duck squawked, and soon there was a deafening roar of ducks quacking.

St. Peter appeared with an ugly woman and asked, "Who stepped on a duck?"

"I did," admitted one of the men. St. Peter immediately pulled out a pair of handcuffs and cuffed the man to the homely woman. "I told you not to step on the ducks," he said. "Now you'll be handcuffed together for eternity."

The two other men were very cautious not to step on any ducks, but a couple of weeks later, one of them accidentally did. The quacks were as deafening as before, and within minutes, St. Peter walked up with a woman who was even uglier than the other one. He determined who stepped on the duck by seeing the fear in the man's face, and he cuffed him to the woman.

"I told you not to step on the ducks," St. Peter said. "Now you'll be handcuffed together for eternity."

The third man was now extra careful. Some days he wouldn't even move for fear of nudging a duck. After three months of this, he still hadn't stepped on a duck.

Then, out of the blue, St. Peter walked up to the man with the most beautiful woman the man had ever seen. St. Peter smiled and without a word, handcuffed him to the beautiful woman and walked off.

The man, knowing that he would be handcuffed to this woman for eternity, let out a sigh and said, "What have I done to deserve this?"

The woman replied, "I don't know about you, but I stepped on a duck."

Teddy Bears

Rory McIlroy met his ex-fiancée Caroline Wozniacki at a tennis tournament.

Rory knew about her stamina and her reputation for having an incredible sex drive, and was excited when she invited him back to her place.

At her apartment there were hundreds of teddy bears. There were many small bears on a low shelf, medium sized ones on a shelf a little higher, and some big fluffy bears on the top shelf.

Rory was surprised at Caroline's extensive collection of teddy bears, but decides not to mention it as she puts some sexy, seductive music on.

They start to kiss, and before long they have ripped each other's clothes off and are making love.

After an intense hour of passion, Rory rolls over, smiles and asks, "Well, how was it?"

Caroline looks him in the eye and replies, "You can have any prize from the bottom shelf."

Three Dogs

A doctor, an architect, and an attorney were dining at the country club one day, and they began to discuss their respective dogs, which were apparently quite extraordinary. A bet was placed to establish who had the most intelligent dog.

The doctor showed his dog first, and called out, "Hippocrates, come." Hippocrates ran in, and was told by the doctor to do his stuff. Hippocrates ran to the golf course and dug for a while, producing a number of bones. He carried the bones into the club and then assembled them into a complete human skeleton. The physician patted Hippocrates on the head, and gave him a cookie for his efforts.

The architect called for his dog, "Sliderule, come." Sliderule ran in, and was told to do his stuff. Straight away the dog chewed the skeleton to rubble, and re-assembled the bone fragments into a scale replica model of the Taj Mahal. The architect patted his dog on the head and gave him a cookie.

The attorney called for his dog, "Bullshit, come." Bullshit ran in and was told to do his stuff. Bullshit immediately f*cked the other two dogs, stole their cookies, sold the Taj Mahal replica to the other members for his fee, and then went outside to play golf.

The Desert Island

One day an Irishman, who has been stranded on a desert island for ten years, looks out to sea and sees a strange dot on the horizon.

He thinks to himself, "It's not a ship."

As the speck begins to get closer, he rules out the possibilities of it being a small boat, then even a raft.

Ultimately, a stunningly beautiful woman wearing a wet suit and scuba gear comes out of the beach onto the island.

She approaches the speechless castaway and says, "How long has it been since you've had a cigarette?"

He replies, "Ten long years."

With that, she unzips a waterproof pocket on her left arm and pulls out a pack of cigarettes.

He takes one, lights it, takes a drag and pronounces, "Sweet Jesus. That is good."

She looks at him and asks, "How long has it been since you've tasted Irish Whiskey?"

Trembling, the Irishman answers, "Ten long years."

She then unzips a sleeve on her right arm, pulls out a hipflask and passes it to him.

He opens the flask, takes a gulp and declares, "Faith and begorah. That is absolutely fantastic."

She then begins to slowly unzip the long zipper that runs down the front of her wet suit, smiles seductively and asks, "How long has it been since you've played around?"

With tears in his eyes, the Irishman falls to his knees and weeps, "Holy Moses, don't tell me you've got a set of golf clubs in there."

Trumped

Donald Trump and his Secretary of Defense are assigned to two senior caddies at an exclusive country club.

The older of the two caddies says, "It is a real honor to be caddying for you gentlemen and may I ask what prompted you to come to our course?"

The senator replies, "We're formulating plans for an attack on the Middle East."

The other caddie says, "Crikey, what's going to happen?"

Trump replies, "We're going to kill 10 million Muslims and a blonde with big tits."

The senior caddie says, "A blonde with big tits? Why kill a blonde a blonde with big tits?"

Trump turns to his defense secretary and says, "See, I told you, no-one gives a damn about the 10 million Muslims."

Chewing Gum

After missing the cut in a tournament Tiger Woods is in the clubhouse talking to Sergio Garcia who is busy chewing gum.

Sergio says, "You Americans are so fat. You eat too much bread."

Tiger says, "Yes, we eat bread. But we Americans eat the inside of the bread and take the outside and recycle it to make cereal for Spain."

Sergio chews on his gum and says, "You Americans eat too many bananas."

Tiger says, "Yes, we eat bananas. But we Americans eat the inside of the bananas and take the outside and recycle it to make smoothies for Spain."

Sergio chews on his gum and says, "You Americans do not know how to have safe sex."

Tiger says, "Yes, we enjoy safe sex. But we Americans use condoms and when we finish with them we recycle them and make chewing gum for Spain."

The Genie In The Bottle

A married couple are playing golf, when the wife has a wild tee shot, which flies off into a villa adjoining the course, breaking a window.

The couple approach the house and knock on the door.

Hearing no answer and seeing that the door is open, they go inside.

Entering the beautiful house they notice her golf ball lying next to a broken bottle near the broken window.

A distinguished middle-aged gentleman introduces himself to them saying, "Thank you for freeing me. I am a genie, and I have been living in that bottle for five thousand years. For freeing me, I can grant three wishes – one for each of you, and the third is up to me."

The husband without even thinking about it says, "I want a million dollars."

His wife declares, "I want a wardrobe full of designer dresses."

The man says, "So be it. Your wishes are granted."

He continues, "My desire is to have sex with the lady present. After five thousand years of abstinence I hope you will understand."

The husband and wife agree since their extravagant wishes had been granted.

So the wife goes upstairs for a marathon sex session.

Lying in bed afterwards, the woman is asked, "How old are you and your husband?"

She replies breathlessly, "We're both thirty years old, but why are you asking?"

He says, "Well, you think by now you would have stopped believing in genies."

Confession

A man goes to confession and says, "Forgive me father for I have sinned."

The priest asks if he would like to confess his sins and the man replies that he used the 'F-word' over the weekend.

The priest says, "Just say three Hail Marys and try to watch your language."

The man replies that he would like to confess as to why he said the 'F-word.'

The priest sighs deeply and tells him to continue.

He says, "Well Father, I played golf on Sunday with my buddies instead of going to church."

The priest says, "And you got upset over that and swore?"

The man replied, "No, that wasn't why I swore. On the first tee I hooked my drive left into the trees."

The priest asked, "And that's when you swore?"

The man replied, "No, it wasn't. When I walked up the fairway, I noticed my ball had got a lucky bounce and I had a clear shot to the green. However, before I could hit the ball, a squirrel ran by and grabbed my ball and scurried up a tree."

The priest asked, "Is that when you said the 'F-word'?"

The man replied, "No, because an eagle then flew by and picked up the squirrel in its talons and flew away."

The priest let out a breath and queried, "Is that when you swore?"

The man replied, "No, because the eagle flew over the green and the dying squirrel let go of my golf ball and it landed 6 inches from the hole."

The priest shrieked, "Don't tell me you missed the f*cking putt!"

Four Old Codgers

A sexy blonde is standing by the first tee waiting for her golf lesson from the pro.

A fourball is in the process of teeing off. The first golfer hits his drive 200 yards straight down the middle of the fairway.

"That was a good shot," said the blonde. "Not bad considering my impediment," said the golfer. "What's wrong with you?" said the blonde. "I have a glass eye," said the golfer. "I don't believe you, show me," said the blonde. He popped his eye out and showed her.

The next golfer hits his drive 210 yards straight down the middle of the fairway. "That was a good shot," said the blonde. "Not bad considering my impediment," said the golfer. "What's wrong with you?" said the blonde. "I have a prosthetic arm," said the golfer. "I don't believe you, show me," said the blonde, so he screwed his arm off and showed her.

The next golfer hits his drive 220 yards straight down the middle of the fairway. "That was a good shot," said the blonde. "Not bad considering my impediment," said the golfer. "What's wrong with you?" said the blonde. "I have a prosthetic leg," said the golfer. "I don't believe you, show me," said the blonde, so he screwed his leg off and showed her.

The fourth golfer hits his drive 230 yards straight down the middle of the fairway. "That was a good shot," said the blonde. "Not bad considering my impediment," said the golfer. "What's wrong with you?" said the blonde. "I have an artificial heart," said the golfer. "I don't believe you, show me," said the blonde.

"I can't show you out here in the open," said the golfer. "Let's go behind the Pro Shop."

As they had not returned within five minutes, his golfing partners decided to go and see what was holding them up.

As they looked behind the Pro Shop, sure enough, there was the golfer, screwing his heart out.

The Lodger

Mike and Ellie took on a 19 year old girl as a lodger.

She asked if she could have a bath but Ellie told her they didn't have a bathroom and she could use their tin bath which was in front of the fire.

"Monday is the best night, when my husband goes out for drinks with his buddies from the golf club," she said, so the girl agreed to have a bath the following Monday.

The next Monday, after her husband had gone to the golf club for a pint with the boys, Ellie filled the bath and watched as the lodger got undressed.

She was surprised to see that the lass didn't have any pubic hair at all, and she told Mike about this when he came home.

Mike didn't believe his wife so she said, "Next week I'll leave a gap in the curtains so that you can see for yourself."

The following Monday, while the girl again got undressed, Ellie asked, "Do you shave?"

"Yes," replied the girl. "I like to keep it clean shaven. What about you? Do you have hair down there?"

"Oh yes I do", said Ellie and she showed off her great mound of bushy pubes.

Late, when Mike got back home Ellie asked him, "Did you see the lodger's muff?"

"Yes," he replied, "but why did you have to show her yours?"

"What's the problem?" she said, "You've seen it many times before."

"I know", he said, "but my f***ing golfing buddies hadn't."

Reading The Line

Three guys, Andy, Brian and Carlo go out to play a round of golf.

Just before Andy tees off, this beautiful woman walks up carrying her clubs.

She says her partner didn't show and asks if she can join them.

All the guys agreed. The woman says, "I don't care what the three of you do; you can, swear, smoke, spit, fart or whatever. Just don't try to coach me on my game."

The guys say okay and ask if she would like to tee off first. All eyes are on her ass as her skirt rides up when she bends over to place the ball

She then proceeds to knock the ball right down the middle. She starts pounding these guys, parring every hole.

They get to the 18th and she has a 15-foot putt for par.

She turns around and says, "You guys have done a great job at not trying to coach me on my game. I've never shot par before, and I'm going to ask your opinions on this putt. Now if any of your opinions help me make the putt, I will give that guy a blow job he will never forget."

The guys all agree it's a great deal.

Andy walks over, eyes up the putt and says, "Lady, aim that putt six inches to the right of the hole. The ball will break left 12 inches from the hole and drop into the cup."

Brian walks up and says, "I think you should aim 12 inches to the right and the ball will break left two feet from the hole and fall into the cup."

Carlo looks at both of them in disgust, walks over, picks up the ball, drops it into the cup, unzips his fly and says, "That's a gimme sweetheart."

Second Wife

A husband and wife are lying quietly in bed reading when the wife looks over at him and asks a question.

Wife: "Would you get married again if I died?"

Husband: "Definitely not, honey."

Wife: "Why not? Don't you like being married?"

Husband: "Of course I do."

Wife: "Then why wouldn't you remarry?"

Husband: "Okay, okay, - I'd get married again."

Wife: "Would you live in our house?"

Husband: "Sure - it's a great house."

Wife: "Would you sleep with her in our bed?"

Husband: "Where else would we sleep darling?"

Wife: "Would you replace my pictures with hers?"

Husband: "That would seem like the proper thing to do."

Wife: "Would you take her golfing with you?"

Husband: "Yes - Those are always good times."

Wife: "Would she use my clubs?"

Husband: "'No, she's left-handed."

Silence.

Husband: "Oh Damn!"

Arm Transplant

A keen golfer was involved in a car crash and was rushed to the hospital.

"I have some good news and some bad news," the surgeon told him. "The bad news is that I will have to remove your right arm."

"Oh God no, my golfing days will be over." cries the man. "So what is the good news?"

The surgeon replies, "The good news is I have another arm to replace it with, but it's a woman's arm and I will need your permission before I can go ahead with the transplant."

The man says, "If it means I can play golf again, go for it, Doc."

The operation went well and a year later the man went in for a check-up.

"How's the new arm?" asks the surgeon.

"Just great," says the golfer. "I'm playing the best golf of my life, my new arm has a much finer touch."

"Not only that," he continued, "I've learned how to iron, my handwriting has improved and I've taken up painting landscapes in watercolors."

The surgeon said, "I'm so glad to hear the transplant was a success. Are you having any side effects?"

"Well, just two" said the golfer, "I have trouble parking the car and, every time I get an erection, I also get a headache."

Four Sons

Four men were due to play golf, and three had arrived and while they were waiting on the fourth to show up they started discussing their children.

The first man told the others how his son had started working as a used car salesman, but now owns a car dealership and is doing so well, that last year he gave a friend a brand new car as a gift.

The second man said that his son has his own construction firm having started work as a bricklayer's apprentice and he's doing so well that last year he was able to give a good friend of his a brand-new home.

The third man boasts that his son has worked his way up through a stock trading company, and is now so successful that in the last month he gave a good friend a large amount of shares in IBM as a gift.

As the fourth man joins them, the other three guys inform him that they have been discussing how successful their respective sons are, and are curious to find out how his son is getting on.

He says, "Actually I'm not pleased with how my son has turned out. For many years he has been a hairdresser, and he recently told me that he is gay."

He continued, "However, looking on the bright side, he must be good at what he does, because his last three boyfriends have given him a car, a brand new house and some shares in IBM."

Lost In Translation

An American guy travels to Tokyo on business.

One night, he's feeling a little frisky so he goes to a geisha bar. After a few drinks, he hires one of the women to go back to his hotel for some action.

While they are having sex, she begins moaning, then screaming. As she catches her breath, she begins shouting, "Machigatta ana! Machigatta ana!"

The guy doesn't speak any Japanese, but he is really enjoying it, and speeds up a bit as she keeps screaming, "Machigatta ana! Machigatta ana!"

After they are done, he pays her, and she leaves, barely able to walk out of the room.

The next day, he is playing golf with an executive at the Japanese company he had been meeting with.

Incredibly, he manages a hole in one.

He doesn't know any Japanese so he yells, "Machigatta ana! Machigatta ana!"

The Japanese guy he is playing with stares at him and asks, "What do you mean, wrong hole?"

Chapter 7: Rude Phrases In Golf

The game of golf lends itself to all kinds of filthy phrases. How many of these have you heard before?

I think I need to change my grip.

I tugged it a little.

My hands are so sweaty I can't get a good grip.

After 18 holes I can barely walk.

I have a stiff shaft.

I'm going to wash my balls.

Grip it softly and stroke it smoothly.

He snuck that in the back door.

It looks pretty wet down there.

You can either bang it in hard or slip it in gently.

Shall we make it a threesome?

That's a hole to be respected.

My shaft is bent.

It's important to have clean balls.

I've had too many strokes.

I've got incredible length.

You really whacked the hell out of that sucker.

Nice stroke, but your follow through has a lot to be desired.

I just shaved the hole.

Keep your head down and spread your legs a bit.

I really enjoyed that threesome/foursome.

Chapter 8: The Rules of Bedroom Golf

1) Each player shall furnish his own equipment for play: one club and two balls.

2) Play on a course must be approved by the owner of the hole.

3) Course owners reserve the right to restrict club length to avoid damage to the hole.

4) For most effective play, the club should have a firm shaft. Course owners are permitted to check shaft stiffness before play begins.

5) Unlike outdoor golf, the object is to get the club in the hole and keep the balls out of the hole.

6) Course owners may request that balls be cleaned before beginning play.

7) The object of the game is to take as many strokes as necessary until the course owner is satisfied that play is complete. Failure to do so may result in being denied permission to play the course again.

8) It is considered bad form to begin playing the hole immediately upon arrival at the course. The experienced player will take time to admire the entire course, with special attention to well-formed bunkers.

9) Players are warned not to mention other courses on which they have played.

10) Players are encouraged to bring proper rain gear for their own protection.

11) If a player frequently misses the hole and lands in the surrounding rough, it is acceptable to ask the course owner for guidance.

12) Players should assure themselves that their match has been properly scheduled, particularly when a new course is being played for the first time.

13) Players should not assume a course is in shape for play at all times. Sometimes the course may be temporarily under repair. Players are advised to be extremely tactful in this situation.

14) Players are advised to obtain the course owner's permission before attempting to play the back nine.

15) Players should take care when playing water hazards, as course owners often don't appreciate wet spots on the course.

16) In contrast to outdoor golf, very few players find hitting balls hard to be very satisfying.

17) Slow play is encouraged. However players should be prepared to proceed at a quicker pace at the course owner's request.

18) It is unusual for a course owner to allow foursomes to play, and when they do, the players usually don't tee off at the same time.

19) Players assume all risk when playing on courses that charge green fees.

20) If a player is unable to locate a course upon which to play, it is OK for him to practice his strokes by himself.

Chapter 9: Why Golf Is Better Than Sex

It's perfectly respectable to golf with a total stranger.

Your golf partner won't keep asking questions about other partners you've played with.

You don't have to sneak your golf magazines into the house.

If you are having trouble with golf, it is perfectly acceptable to pay a professional to show you how to improve your technique.

If your partner takes pictures or films you golfing, you don't have to worry about them showing up on the Internet.

When you see a really good golfer, you don't have to feel guilty about imagining the two of you golfing together.

If your regular golf partner isn't available, he/she won't object if you golf with someone else.

Nobody will ever tell you that you will go blind if you golf by yourself.

Nobody expects you to give up golfing if your partner loses interest in the game.

You can have a golf calendar on your wall at the office.

There is no such thing as a golfing transmitted disease.

Nobody expects you to promise to golf with just one partner for the rest of your life.

The Ten Commandments don't say anything about golf.

If you want to watch golf on television, you don't have to subscribe to a premium TV channel.

You don't have to go to a sleazy shop in a seedy neighborhood to buy golf stuff.

You don't have to be a newlywed to plan a vacation primarily for the enjoyment of golf.

Your golf partner will never say, "We had golf last week. Is that all you ever think about?"

Chapter 10: Golf Slang

Golfers can be quite creative when describing some of their shots, or their partner's shots. Try and remember some of these for when you are out playing in the next few weeks.

Slang - Tee Shots

A Sally Gunnell	Ugly to look at, but a good runner
A Glenn Miller	Didn't make it over the water
An O.J. Simpson	Got away with it
A Gay Midget	It's low and it sucks
A Princess Grace	Should have taken a driver
A Princess Diana	Shouldn't have taken a driver
A Robert Downey Jr	A real snorter
A Condom	Safe but unsatisfying
A Posh Spice	Too thin
A Danny DeVito	Short and fat
A Giraffe's Arse	High and shitty
A Pavarotti	Sounded great but died
A Lindsay Lohan	Started straight but bent into the rough

Slang - Approach Shots

A Kate Winslet	A bit fat, but not too bad
A Kate Moss	A bit thin
A German Virgin	Guten tight – close to the pin
A Marc Bolan	Hit a tree
A Nipple Licker	A shot that opens up the hole
A Yasser Arafat	Ugly and in the sand
A Rick Waller	One club too many
A Jo Brand	Fat and ugly
A Beyoncé	Chunky but on the dance floor
A Rodney King	Overclubbed
A Roseanne Barr	Fat and short
A Bin Laden	In the water, lost forever
A Vinnie Jones	Got a nasty kick
An Anna Kournikova	Looks great, but unlikely to get a result
A mother-in-law	It looks good when it's leaving
A son-in-law	Not what you wanted but it will have to do
A sister-in-law	You're up there although you know you shouldn't be

Slang - Putting

A Rock Hudson	Thought it was straight but it wasn't
A Joe Pesci	A mean little five footer
A Danny DeVito	An ugly little five footer
A Diego Maradona	A nasty little five footer
A Monica Lewinsky	Lip out, but no hole
A Brazilian	Shaves the hole
An Elton John	A big bender that lips the rim
The Junior Prom	All lip, no hole
Lipstick on a pig	Holing a long putt after some previous dross

She had it in her mouth and then her dad walked in....

A putt that lips out after doing 180 degrees around the cup.

Slang - On the course

A Paris Hilton	An expensive hole
A Simon Cowell	Needs to be hit really hard
Cream on sh*t	Scrambling a par after many bad shots
A Ladyboy	Looks like an easy hole but all is not what it seems

Chapter 11: Golfers Pick-Up Lines

I have a stiff shaft.

Keep your head down and spread your legs a bit.

I'm looking for a new partner for regular match ups.

From the moment I saw you, I've had a vertical shaft angle.

Fancy a foursome?

I have a pretty good swing.

Are you a water hazard? Because you've got me soaking wet.

Let's go swinging together sometime.

My balls have dimples.

Which do you prefer? Stroke Play or Skins?

I hope you like it rough.

Are you into kinky stuff? I'll let you beat me.

Do you want me to pull it?

Hey baby, can you suck a golf ball through 50 feet of garden hose?

I can grip it and rip it.

I am strong with my approach play.

How many strokes do you want?

Are you looking for the fairway? Because you coming back to mine is the only fair way for this evening to go.

My balls are always clean.

I have a long shaft.

It looks pretty wet down there.

About The Author

Chester Croker, known to his friends as Chester the Jester, has written many joke books, and has twice been named Comedy Writer of the Year by the International Jokers Guild. In over 30 years playing golf, Chester has met many funny characters that have helped provide him with plenty of material for this book.

Hopefully, this book has added a few gems to your repertoire of dirty golf jokes, and if you see anything wrong in this book, or have a gag you would like to see included in the next version of the book, please visit the glowwormpress.com website.

If you enjoyed the book, please review it on Amazon so that other golfers can have a good laugh too.

The final word – Even when the game is getting you down, golf is the most fun you can have without taking your clothes off. Also, let's remember that golf is a game invented by the same people who think music comes out of a bagpipe.

Printed in Great Britain
by Amazon

24819269R00078